The Secret L

The Secret Life of Rose

Foreword by Dr Luke Beardon

Being in a position of privilege is such a privilege. I am one of the luckiest people I am aware of in that I get so many autistic insights from all sorts of people from all walks of life. Each and every insight is another layer of wonder for me, and just that bit more of added illumination into the autistic lived experience. And you – you lucky, privileged reader – now get to read some of the amazing experiences from Rose and Jodie, the wonderful duo who have opted to share some words of reality 'through the autism lens' about what it is really like to be autistic.

Rose gives us an astonishingly clear narrative on a range of topics from stimming to meltdown to masking to sensory issues to her unique skill set while Jodie offers her perspective on how Rose's experiences might be understood in a broader sense. Deeply personal, and definitely personable, this well written prose deserves a wide readership.

Both Rose and Jodie provide such honest opinions which go some way towards dispelling those pesky autism myths; it was refreshing to say the least to read about Rose's empathic abilities! It is impressive how many gems of wisdom are packed into this book; I found myself devouring it at speed – and immediately returning to the beginning to allow myself more time to digest
what I was reading.

Thank you Rose – for sharing your (not so) secret life! I have no doubt whatsoever that in doing so you will touch many other lives in a positive way. And Jodie – your final words on 'AUtism is AUsome' are a fantastic finale to a fantastic book.

The Secret Life of Rose

Introduction

My name is Rose and I am eleven years old. I am autistic and I found this out when I was ten.

The reason I'm writing this book is because I want people to understand autism from my perspective. This means that I will be telling you about my autism and how it affects me.

I hope that some of the things I do in life to help me will also help you. I also hope that by hearing about me you will understand yourself or someone you know better.

I have a YouTube channel which is also called 'The Secret Life of Rose' - please take a look if you would like to know more after reading this book.

I am Rose's mum. I work as an independent autism specialist when Rose was 6 I realised what we often saw in her were autistic traits. Having her formally identified as autistic was somewhat of a struggle: Rose's autism was not visible and was more evident in her Ausomeness rather than the 'deficits' required for an identification. I am hoping that my experience as a parent and a practitioner will support your journey of discovery, which actually never really ends!

The book is laid out into sections chosen by Rose and myself. Each one covers an aspect of Rose's experiences as an autistic child. After Rose's voice comes the 'adult' bit to offer a broader view of the autistic experience.

Jodie Smitten
BSc Psy. PgC Autism. MBPsS.

Children's Well-being Practitioner
Specialising In Autism

A few words about words

You may have noticed we use the word 'identification', whereas some may use the word 'diagnosis'. For us the word 'diagnosis' reminds us of a doctor telling someone they are ill! We often talk about 'discovering' being autistic rather than being diagnosed with it. We like the word discovery – it makes us think of something exciting, a journey of discovery!

For similar reasons we talk about being autistic rather than 'having autism'. Again, we don't 'have' an illness, like we have chickenpox or scabies! Autism isn't something that requires treatment – it is a person's identity.

What is Autism?

Rose

Autism means that your brain works differently than someone who isn't autistic. Even if someone else is autistic your brain will still work differently to theirs. For example, they may react differently to certain things compared to you: they may hate tight clothes and you may love them.

My brain sees the world in a different way. Sometimes you might feel you belong on a different planet. I sometimes feel like I belong on a planet where people jump about the whole time.

Sometimes an autistic brain can malfunction, meaning the person may have a meltdown, lose their appetite or feel they can't speak. The reason for this is there is so much going on that your brain can't take it all in at once anymore. You can sometimes cope for a bit but then your brain gets full and starts to overflow.

There is a bright side of autism, such as you might have a really good memory, you could be really good at a certain subject or skill. Some autistic people can understand other people's emotions really well and get how they feel.

Autism is different perspective on the world, a different way of sensing what's around you. Very often this sense leads to a mind full of wonder and amazement. Taking in the world in such an intense way means that overload can easily be reached at times. However this can also result in experiencing incredible levels of joy.

The autistic children I have the pleasure to know offer me the most incredible insight into how their minds work and I'm forever grateful for all they teach me. They are the bravest, most interesting and kind humans you could meet. Autism leads to struggles at times, many of which can be adjusted for and avoided if the people around them are able to reframe and respond with nurture.

With the correct support and love your child will reach more than many doctors would have you believe!

There is a saying that goes, 'Sometimes you have to forget what you thought life would be and appreciate what you have got.' On discovering you have an autistic child this should read, 'You have to forget what you thought would be, as the journey you will go on will enable growth beyond what you could imagine.'

Having an autistic child and supporting so many families has made me a better parent, a better person and actually given me an incredibly deep insight into myself. You can achieve this too.

The Secret Life of Rose

Stimming

Rose

Stimming is an action or a noise that you repeat over and over again when you are excited, worried or angry.

This could be jumping up and down, making lots of random noises, clapping your hands, flapping your arms, chewing things, kicking your legs, biting your nails, biting your lip, fiddling with your hair, repeating phrases from the TV, saying the same word over and over again, rocking backwards and forwards, bouncing, picking, watching the same bit of a TV show over and over again, opening of mouth into unusual poses, standing on your head, talking in accents or a baby voice and many, many more.

Stimming helps me to let out energy, to focus and concentrate, and to feel more calm and chilled.

You shouldn't worry about stimming; you should just do it!

(Although you may want to explain to your friends what it's all about!)

Stimming makes me feel zoned out of the world and I can only think of the thing I am happy about – it blocks anything else out.

If I'm stimming because I'm not feeling good, like if I'm nervous, then flapping my hands or fiddling with something distracts me from the bad feelings and blocks them out.

Stimming (self-stimulatory behaviours) is way of regulating emotions, good or bad. Stimming should never be disallowed or disciplined. If it causes harm to someone such as skin picking/self-harm then a replacement stim offering similar sensory feedback should be explored. Stimming should never be discouraged due to fear of judgement from others; instead, onlookers should have stimming explained to them.

Stimming is an expression or communication of emotion, and emotions should always be embraced.

It's helpful to take note of stims and when they occur. Determining if a stim indicates distress or excitement means you can act accordingly; for example, if your child is communicating distress then you can support them by removing them from the source of distress. If a child is expressing enjoyment then you make mental note of what your child is experiencing and give more opportunity to engage in this. Stimming behaviours are closely lined with sensory profiles of autistic people; therefore, it can be helpful for both parents and children to be aware of their own stims and to use them as coping tools in managing emotions.

The Secret Life of Rose

Masking

> ### Rose
>
> Masking is when you're upset or angry or worried and you act like you are happy. It can also mean  that you act and behave like other children in your surroundings but I don't tend to do this as much, because my friends seem to accept who I am even though I am different from them. Although I don't often stim in front of them.
>
> When I mask, at the end of the day it makes me feel worn out because you're acting an emotion that you are not actually feeling. To do it I just pretend like nothing has happened to upset me and I just smile and carry on as normal. I keep the feelings of upset inside.
>
> To help me show my feelings, at school I have a card: one side is red and the other is green. When I

am upset or worried or angry I turn it to show the red side. Then I get to go outside onto the playground and kick around my football for 5 minutes – this makes me feel calmer because I am focusing on the ball and not on how I'm feeling. It also gives me a break from the classroom which helps.

When I was younger I was scared to use the card because I thought people might ask me questions about it and wonder what it is. I was also worried that teachers might ask me what was wrong and I can't tell people about how I'm feeling. People know now that I have it and why I have it. Teachers and children in my class now know I am autistic and that has been a good thing for me.

Masking is incredibly common within the autistic community. Masking is a suppression of self; emotions, interests, needs and identity. Masking is often subconscious and is a strategy that develops to protect the individual from harm, ridicule, discipline, uncomfortable attention, questions or comments and bullying. Essentially it is a survival strategy to manage the non-autistic world.

It's vital that parents and professionals are aware of masking. If you are a parent whose child is well-behaved in school and lets it all out on you at home, it can be hard to access assessments and support.

Children should be supported to unmask in the safety of those who know and love them. When others become accepting of their differences, autistic children feel more able to unmask at school and with friends.

The Secret Life of Rose

Sensory Experiences

Rose

For me, 'sensory' means some things feel really horrible (itchy clothes, like tights) and some things feeling really nice (baggy clothes and rollercoasters).

We have eight senses. Five are the ones everyone knows: touch, smell, hearing/sounds, taste and sight. The other ones my mum will talk about!

Touch: Anyone touching me at all feels weird – I usually have to 'wipe' it away to take away the feeling. My legs are really ticklish, even if someone gently touches them. It's not a nice funny ticklish feeling, it's horrible and makes me upset and uncontrollably kick out. I don't do hugs or kisses even with my parents, because it feels tingly, which is not nice. I do high fives instead.

Touch also means I find some clothes really uncomfortable. I don't like tight clothes including tights, jeans, trousers, dresses, skirts, some socks, belts, tight tops. In fact all I like to wear is comfy, soft, baggy clothes like jogging bottoms, sports leggings, football kits, lose T-shirts and sometimes jumpsuits. I don't like girly clothes and prefer boyish style.

Touch also impacts my hair. I hate having it cut. I will only wear it in one style, a high ponytail, as otherwise it touches my skin on my neck which makes me itchy.

Getting wet is an odd one – I like swimming pools and hot tubs but I don't like showers or baths. I think it is because most showers or baths are quite small and I don't like small spaces. The problem with getting wet is that you have to get dry after. The issue with doing this is that the sensation of the towel on my skin feels scratchy so I tend to dry myself by waving the towel around me and sometimes even using the hairdryer.

Noise: I don't like other people shouting, it hurts my ears, making them feel like they will explode.

I actually like making loud

noises myself, I find it funny. It makes me excited, but also calms me as it lets all my energy out.

I really HATE it when people use complicated words or lots of words when they are explaining things to me because I can't understand what they are trying to say. Too many words confuse and overwhelm me and can make me have a meltdown or shutdown.
Noise around me being made by other people or things when I'm trying to concentrate is very annoying because I can't focus on what I'm doing, I can only focus on the noise. This affects me at school and at home as it can even make watching TV hard.

Smells: I don't really have much to say about smells, they don't bother me too much. Although I do really like the smell of lemon and lime.

Taste/Food Texture:
I don't like foods all mixed up or touching each other. For example, when we have a roast dinner I have separate piles for different foods and I

eat them separately e.g. all the carrots then all the chicken. I tend to eat the piles in a certain order. I don't eat things like chilli or spaghetti bolognaise where everything is mixed together.

I can really like a food and want to eat it all the time and then I will suddenly go off of it. This can annoy my parents as they buy lots of what I like and then I don't want it anymore!

I mostly eat different meals to others in my family. My meals are usually the same each day.

Choosing what to eat is annoying because I never know what I want, even if I look in the fridge and cupboards. This can make me feel really stressed. Having to eat is annoying as it just feels like so much effort. Unless its sweets and chocolate!!

Foods I don't like make me feel sick and the thought of eating them is gross. Really gross.

Making me eat foods I don't like is not nice at all. No-one should have to eat something that makes them feel sick or that they find gross.

I sometimes feel like I need to eat all the time. But sometimes I don't want to eat at all!

Visual: I'm good at noticing small details; I'm great at spot the difference games, although I do struggle to find things I have lost, especially amongst mess (e.g. my bedroom!!!).

Movement and Play wrestling! As I said in stimming, I love moving, jumping, bouncing and clapping my hands. I also love play fighting and going to my dad's homemade gym. Play fighting helps me to make a decision when I am struggling too- this happens a lot. After play fighting I am able to decide.

Chewing things helps me concentrate on school work.

Lifting heavy things in the gym makes me feel more energised and ready for the day. Some mornings I can feel like a slug. When I feel like this I am very slow-moving; I don't know what to do and can't make any decisions, and this sometimes makes me feel tired. Play fighting or jumping on the trampoline can help me to feel less slug-like.

Inner Sensations; sometimes I don't really know I need the loo until I'm desperate. I'm not sure I want to tell people about going to the toilet!!

I don't know if I feel pain differently to others as I don't know how others feel pain! But I do seem to find small cuts very painful, but big scrapes with blood not painful at all!

Sometimes I don't feel pain until I see the injury!

Sometimes I am hungry ALL the time; sometimes I forget to eat all day and don't feel hungry at all!

I don't cope well when it is hot – it feels like loads of needles stabbing into me.

Sensory sensitivities can be one of the biggest causes of anxiety and overwhelm. We cannot underestimate the levels of distress sensory experiences can cause. I would like to emphasise the point that all children should be believed when expressing distress: it's all too easy to discount a sensation that you don't find relatable. Sensory discomfort can be excruciatingly painful.

Sensory seeking behaviours such as constant movement, fiddling, chewing, and making noises are types of stimming. A child is using these to naturally re-regulate or produce joyful feelings and so as parents it's great to take a note of what your child is doing to form the basis of a sensory diet, i.e. providing and encouraging opportunities for your child to experiences these sensations throughout the day and/or when becoming distressed to settle them. As with stimming, both sensory avoidance and sensory seeking are forms of communication. Listen to what your child is communicating and respond appropriately.

Sensory profiles change over time, and children can experience heightened sensitivity during times of anxiety. If your child is seemingly more agitated with their clothing than normal or more 'picky' with food, this is likely them communicating that they feel unsettled about something else going on for them. Always be curious as to what is going on for your child and unpick that with them when they are feeling calm.

The 3 senses that are less well known are:

Proprioception; the sense that tells us where our body is in space and what is doing.

Vestibular; sensations of body rotation, gravitation, balance and movement that stem from the inner ear.

> *Interoception; our inner sensations that advise us on when our basic needs want attention. These include toileting, eating, drinking, and staying warm/not overheating, sleeping and emotional regulation.*

Proprioception *is an amazing sense. Proprioceptive sensory experiences are fantastic for calming an anxious, unsettled, overwhelmed child, as well as one in a sluggish/shutdown/low energy state. Proprioception is a sensory experience that offers high levels of input on the body such as pushing, pulling, being squashed, trampolining and carrying heavy items. We spend a lot of time play wrestling or doing weights with Rose at various intervals throughout the day. These activities help maintain functional levels of energy and manage her anxiety.*

Interoception *is really important to be aware of. Simply put, it is our inner sensations that indicate to us what basic needs need to be met. This includes hunger, thirst, needing the toilet, needing to sleep and indicating pain. Sensory differences mean that autistic people can be both hypersensitive to these signals, e.g. feeling starving at the first twinge of hunger, and hyposensitive, e.g. not realising you need the loo until you are desperate and then you struggle to get there in time!*

Interoception differences also impact emotions, which we cover in the next section.

Vestibular *seeking children are the ones who love swings, going upside down and can spin for hours with little sensation of being dizzy. Whereas those who are sensitive are more likely to suffer motion sickness and be fearful of being too far from the ground even when being picked up by an adult.*

Emotions

Rose

I am either really happy or really angry, sad or worried. I can tell them apart but only when they are really strong. This means I don't always know what I feel and what I'm upset about.

I don't feel my emotions slowly coming, I just suddenly feel them really strongly. This makes it difficult to calm myself down before I get really cross. It's hard to use any sensory toys to calm myself down because by the time I need them I am too angry to remember I need them and to get them.

Meditation doesn't help me AT ALL because it bores me. Instead I need movement to help me calm. I enjoy bouncing on the trampoline and jumping around the house.

I only know how I feel if the feeling is very strong. This means that often I don't know how I feel. My mum will ask me but I will just say I don't know. If others ask me, I just say I'm fine because it's easier than explaining that I don't know how I feel.

The Secret Life of Rose

Jodie

Recognising emotions is linked to sensory experiences. Interoception is the body's internal signals and sensations that tell us how we are feeling, whether that's how hungry we feel, how cold we feel or how happy we feel. Interoception differences in autism play a vital role in children becoming emotionally dysregulated.

When talking with families about emotions many report a child that goes from 0-100 in a split second. I frequently ask about whether a child's responses to hunger or needing the toilet are similar, for example: your child may not think they need a wee then two seconds later they are bursting or having accidents. Maybe they also struggle to remember to eat or will go from fine to being so ravenous and 'hangry'. These could indicate that your child is hyposensitive to their internal signals (interoception). Equally a child can be hypersensitive and so the feel first pang of hunger can lead to them feeling like they need to eat all the time. Remember that a child's hypo- and hypersensitivities can change from one day to the next! Us parents are very often on the back foot.

Now if we consider this in relation to emotions, some children have no sensation of happy or angry until they are hyperactively bouncing round the room or exploding into an almighty rage. As a child, imagine how scary this must be when one second you feel fine and the next you feel completely overwhelmed and consumed by an anger that is completely outside of your control.

There is also the consideration of alexithymia, which is the inability to recognise, understand and communicate your emotions (or any one of these). This is not unique to autism but is often a co-occurring condition and worth reading up on. The interplay between alexithymia and the interoceptive sense can make emotions feel scary and overwhelming. Awareness of this is vital for supporting your child with their emotions.

Executive Functioning/Organisation

Rose

Organising myself is hard, because I forget stuff a lot. I forget my homework, my football kit, my lunchbox, my school bag – I basically leave things behind wherever I go! I even went swimming once and forgot my swim bag, but then I realised after twenty minutes of standing in the changing rooms that I hadn't forgotten it but had just left it in the car. I had forgotten that I hadn't forgotten it!!!! Ha ha. Even when my mum reminds me, I can forget what she has said seconds after – this is because I sometimes don't even process what she has said. I don't do this on purpose, it's just that I'm thinking about other things all the time.

Tidying up my bedroom is absolutely impossible sometimes because starting jobs when there is lots to do is REALLY hard. It helps me if someone starts the job with me and gives me smaller parts of it to do at a time.

When my bedroom is tidy, everything is put away

and I can't find anything. If I had my way tidying wouldn't even be a word.

Another part of this is that my idea of time can be a bit off, in that I often leave things until the last minute, not realising how long it may take me to do them.

I am very easily distracted. Hang on, just trying to watch something on the telly! I struggle to concentrate, which means I often start something but don't finish it. Anything can distract me, like something around me that catches my eye. At school the older kids have break earlier than us and if I can see them on the field playing football I get distracted from my schoolwork and watch them. In my English room, there are poems on the wall and I'm easily distracted by them and will sit and read them when I should be listening.

Sometimes I can just be staring into space, distracted by the thoughts that are in my head……. Sorry, just need to speak to my dog! Then I realise the teacher has told me to do something. Oddly, sometimes I still know what they have told me to do even though I haven't been listening!

Jodie

A person with executive functioning difficulties can sometimes be deemed lazy or disorganised. Sadly, many are made to feel this way, as those around them don't realise this is actually due to executive functioning challenges and is not a choice. Executive functioning can be impacted by anxiety, stress, autism and ADHD, so if you have a child with one or a combination of these the impact on them day-to-day can be significant.

Executive functioning can impact (amongst other things): working memory, time management, task initiation, staying on task and emotional regulation, switching tasks and transitions. Putting all your energies into one activity can make it hard to then suddenly move to something else. This is linked to monotropism; a theory of autism that suggested tunnel like attention and worth parents reading into.

If you recognise your child struggles with any or all of these, supporting them by breaking tasks down into small chunks, sharing tasks to reduce the mental load, using visuals such as picture timelines or checklists, and setting alarms/external reminders can really help and also possibly offer them some independence.

The Secret Life of Rose

Empathy

Rose

Empathy is knowing how other people feel.

I am good at this. I can notice small changes in how people look and have learnt what this means and how they might feel. When people are sad, they act differently to how they normally act. If it's someone I don't know then I don't know how they feel by looking at them, as I don't know what they look like normally, unless it's really obvious how they are feeling, like if they are really crying.

Sometimes other people's feelings confuse me. This happens a lot when I am watching the TV. All the crying during Britain's Got Talent is annoying because I don't understand why someone would cry at a song.

The Secret Life of Rose

Jodie

Many autistic children are hypersensitive to the emotions of others. It can be almost like a super sense. This enables many autistic people to actually feel the emotions of others. This can be emotionally draining and exhausting. This in turn can lead to children shutting or melting down in response to the emotions of others, particularly if they are unable to offload these emotions through communication. This can lead to the misconception that autistic people have no empathy, as their responses seem inappropriate.

Rose has learnt emotions through studying patterns of behaviour and noticing changes in patterns to peoples' behaviours. When people don't follow these patterns mismatches of understanding can occur.

We witness her confusion during TV shows as she becomes agitated. Rose dislikes and will avoid watching films due to this. Alexithymia, as discussed in our 'Emotions' section, is worth reading up on if this is relatable.

The Secret Life of Rose

Becoming Overwhelmed: Meltdowns

Rose

A meltdown is when I get overwhelmed and start to feel angry. I start shouting, crying and throwing things sometimes. My head feels like it has been overtaken by angriness – I can't control it, it just happens and seems to come out of nowhere.

The things that trigger them are: too many people being around me and talking to me, not understanding what someone is trying to say to me, or a bad day at school. If I have been masking, when I get home my emotions can all burst out as a meltdown.

It helps me if I am left alone and people don't talk to me. If people ask me if I'm okay I get more cross, because it's pretty obvious that I'm not okay. People asking me, 'What's wrong?' can make me feel worse because sometimes I don't even know what's wrong. Saying nothing to me until I start to feel calmer is better. When I'm calmer, someone saying, 'How can I help you?' is good.

Other things that help me are going to a small space and cuddling my favourite soft toy. The screaming and shouting can help me to get it all out. I often feel tired after but also better for letting it all out.

Jodie

Each child differs in terms of supporting a meltdown. Rose has covered the most important point, that a meltdown is a neurological response to a perceived fear and is therefore not within a child's control. Essentially, a meltdown is like a panic attack. Therefore, we must respond accordingly and not punish, shout or escalate. This is particularly difficult when a child is putting themselves or others at risk of harm: as a parent, our fear response can then also be triggered, making us unable to regulate ourselves in order to support and nurture our child. It is the job of us as the parents to practise calmness in our response to meltdowns; this takes some practice. Everyone's safety is essential during this time, and moving items and other children to another space is often better than trying to remove a child in meltdown, as physical contact without consent can be further triggering.

Some children need a trusted adult to be nearby; some prefer to be alone. Some prefer a deep pressure hug or weighted blanket; others prefer no touch whatsoever. We have learnt what works for Rose through conversation during calm times. Many parents have reported to me that their child will follow them when they try to move away their child in meltdown, this is because you are their safe person. For some children, leaving them alone can create further fear and send a message that you don't want to be around them unless they are fine and happy. Again this is only the case for some and some children actually want to be left alone.

The Dos of supporting a meltdown differ between individuals. The Do not's, however apply more generally: Don't ask questions such as "what's wrong? Are you ok?" Don't punish. Don't shout.

Simply nurture in a way you would a distressed newborn baby.

Negative responses to meltdowns which are outside of children's control can lead to negative cycles. Remember, children know right from wrong and child will do right when they can.

```
        Anxiety
           ↓
'I'm a bad person'      Stress Response
Poor self-esteem        Fight/Fright
           ↑                ↓
        Adult Imposed Consequences
```

Jodie Smitten
BSc Psy. PgC Autism. MBPsS.

Children's Well-being Practitioner
Specialising In Autism

Being Overwhelmed: Shutdowns

Rose

This is where you become so overwhelmed that you become like a robot, you hide, you don't talk to anyone even if they talk to you, you don't want anything – you just want to be alone and for people to leave you alone. I am usually still and maybe curled up in a ball. I may sometimes make funny noises such as repetitive groaning if I'm in a safe place.

Things that help me in a shutdown are pretty much the same as when I'm in meltdown. I feel tired afterwards.

The Secret Life of Rose

Friends, Friendships and Socialising

Rose

I don't like making new friends – it's difficult, I'm not sure why. I just find it hard to speak to people I don't know.

I like to be friends with people who have similar likes to me, as then we have something to talk about. If someone doesn't have the same interests as me I don't think I'd have anything to say to them. If someone was into girly stuff they may just want to talk about make-up and doing hair, and I'm not really interested in that, so I wouldn't know what to say.

When I have a friend round I like to have a plan of what we are going to do, because otherwise we may get a bit bored, and I don't like being bored. This would make me worry that my friend is bored and doesn't want to be around me. My plan is usually written out with different sections and things to do, with a timetable at the bottom.

Talking to people I don't know is absolutely the most frightening thing in the whole entire world. If someone speaks to me that I don't know I have to talk back and it feels scary. If my mum is with me it feels a bit better, as my mum will sometimes speak for me. Some people are scarier to speak to than others, like all the teachers at school, except for teachers that I have had taught me and know me, I often go really quiet and can't get my words out – this is weird, as I can actually become unable to talk and my brain can't think.

Jodie

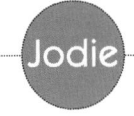

Rose has been mute in some situations since she was a toddler, often acting as though no-one has even said anything to her and redirecting her attention elsewhere. When her sister was born, Rose would often ignore any interaction with an unfamiliar person and simply put her head into the pram and talk to her sister.

Mutism commonly occurs with autism. To ease anxiety a child should never be coaxed into talking or reprimanding for not being able to, as mutism is not a choice. In the case of buying something rose is able to manage independently as she knows this interaction will follow a particular protocol. Social aspects of independence can be practised at home during roleplay. If Rose is embarking on something new independently we talk through the language that will help in the situation. This is important for personal safety. It is important to work out with a child where they would go or what they would say if they needed help when out and about without a familiar adult.

Periods of socialising can lead to exhaustion and a need for recharge in the form of alone time/time on electronics or engaging in their special interests. All of these activities allow the child control and predictability which are much needed after a period of time in unpredictable and exhausting settings.

It's really important that autistic children are given the opportunity to spend time with other autistic children, ideally those that share the same interest. Assuming that an autistic child with get along with any other autistic child is erroneous, but it is important to consider the double empathy problem, introduced by an autistic academic named Damian Milton. The focus of the double empathy problem is that autistic people have social differences, not social "deficits". When autistic people socialise with other autistic people, social differences are not apparent because they share the same social skill set. There is a mutual understanding and acceptance that an autistic person may not encounter when around non-autistics.

Often autistic children naturally gravitate towards each other. Many children I work with have autistic best friends without either of them actually aware of the other's identity. This has all sorts of amazing benefits: they 'get' each other, they feel connected to another individual, they accept each other's quirks, all of which are so good for positive self-identity and mental health.

AUtism is AUsome!!!

Rose

Being autistic means I can do things others can't, like I can remember things from a really long time ago, in detail. I remember the first day back at school in 2015 and we were walking to school, and I felt excited because I would get to write 2015 in my schoolbook instead of 2014. Another time I remember walking to school and it was quite frosty and cold, and we were talking about whether robins come out in the winter – bit random! I often remember conversations.

My great hearing means I'm like a dog, I can hear things that are far away. The best bit about this is I can hear exactly what my mum and dad are saying to each other in the evenings when I'm in bed, even though my bedroom is in the loft!

Being autistic means I'm different from everyone else. This is great, as if you are the same as everyone else it's boring! Knowing you are autistic is even better, as then you don't have to try and be like everyone else, you can just be your own cool, different self. Before I found out I am autistic I felt weird, in a bad way – I thought I had to be like everybody else, and this didn't feel very nice. Now I know I'm autistic I don't have to pretend that I'm the same as everyone else. I'm happier now.

Jodie

Rose and the children I work with are INCREDIBLE. They are creative, resilient, and brave. Every day these little people face a chaotic, unpredictable and uncompromising world! These children constantly have to adapt and adjust their natural ways to suit others.

Their worlds can very quickly and easily become overwhelming and unbearable, but because the non-autistics around them don't have the same experiences they expect the autistic child to just 'get on with it' or 'get over it', and then deem them 'challenging' if they have a meltdown or refuse to engage. Very often these children aren't empathised with – which is ironic, considering the myth around autistic people not having empathy!

I will refer here to the "Golden Equation" coined by Dr Luke Beardon: autism + environment = outcome. For an autistic child to thrive, learn, enjoy life and be free of mental health illnesses it is vital that their world (environment) meets their needs, adjusts to their differences, and not only understands but also accepts who they are.

This is the responsibility of all the adults in their lives, not the child's. We must adjust, we must accept, we must advocate.

Keep being Ausome!!

Rose & Jodie

The Secret Life of Rose

The Secret Life of Rose

The Secret Life of Rose

Printed in Great Britain
by Amazon